# Golden Retrievers

**ABDO**
**Publishing Company**

A Buddy Book
by
Julie Murray

## VISIT US AT

www.abdopub.com

Published by Buddy Books, an imprint of ABDO Publishing Company, 4940 Viking Drive, Suite 622, Edina, Minnesota 55435. Copyright © 2005 by Abdo Consulting Group, Inc. International copyrights reserved in all countries. No part of this book may be reproduced in any form without written permission from the publisher.

Printed in the United States.

Edited by: Christy DeVillier
Contributing Editors: Matt Ray, Michael P. Goecke
Graphic Design: Maria Hosley
Image Research: Deborah Coldiron
Photographs: American Kennel Club, Eyewire Inc., Minden Pictures, Photodisc, PhotoSpin

## Library of Congress Cataloging-in-Publication Data

Murray, Julie, 1969-
    Golden retrievers/Julie Murray.
        p. cm. — (Animal kingdom. Set II)
    Includes bibliographical references (p. ).
    Contents: The dog family — Golden retrievers — What they're like — Coat and color — Size — Care — Feeding — Things they need — Puppies.
    ISBN 1-59197-316-3
        1. Golden retriever—Juvenile literature. [1. Golden retriever. 2. Dogs.] I. Title.

SF429.G63M87 2003
636.752'7—dc21

2002033003

# Contents

The Dog Family ......................................................4

Golden Retrievers ................................................6

What They Look Like ..........................................9

Golden Retrievers As Pets ...............................11

Grooming And Care............................................13

Feeding And Exercise........................................15

Puppies .................................................................19

Dogs With Jobs ..................................................21

Important Words ................................................23

Web Sites .............................................................23

Index .....................................................................24

# The Dog Family

Long ago, all dogs were wild animals. Today, millions of people keep dogs as pets. Dogs are related to foxes, wolves, dingoes, and jackals. They all belong to the Canidae family.

There are many breeds of dogs.

# Golden Retrievers

The American Kennel Club has named about 150 dog **breeds**. A few of them are greyhounds, cocker spaniels, and golden retrievers.

Golden retrievers have been around about 150 years. A man in Scotland had the first golden retrievers. His name was Lord Tweedmouth. He started the golden retriever breed.

Golden retrievers have been around a long time.

People brought golden retrievers to North America in 1894. The American Kennel Club named the **breed** in 1925. Today, golden retrievers are very popular in North America.

Golden retrievers are popular pets.

# What They Look Like

Golden retrievers are medium-sized dogs. They grow to become about 23 inches (58 cm) tall. Adults weigh between 65 and 75 pounds (29 and 34 kg). Female golden retrievers are a bit smaller.

Golden retrievers are medium-sized dogs.

Golden retrievers are gold-colored. Some are light shades of gold. Others are darker shades. Some have golden red coats. Their thick coats may have straight or wavy hair.

This golden retriever has a dark golden red coat.

# Golden Retrievers As Pets

Golden retrievers are strong, active dogs. They make great hunting dogs. Golden retrievers can live indoors or outside.

Some people train their golden retrievers for hunting.

Golden retrievers only need a few baths each year. Too many baths can harm their coat.

Dogs need their nails clipped short. Cleaning a dog's teeth and ears is also important. Ask a **veterinarian** how to do this. A veterinarian is a doctor for animals. Taking pets to a veterinarian helps them stay healthy.

# Feeding And Exercise

All dogs need food and fresh water every day. Adult golden retrievers should be fed once a day. Their food should not change too often. A changing **diet** can lead to health problems.

Give your dog food and water every day.

Golden retrievers are active dogs. They need daily exercise. Owners should take them on long walks. Golden retrievers also enjoy swimming. Playing fetch is also good exercise.

Exercise is good for golden retrievers.

Swimming and playing fetch is great exercise for dogs.

# Chew Toys

Like all dogs, golden retrievers love to chew. Owners can buy special chew toys for them. Rawhides and nylon bones are good chew toys. Chewing these toys helps dogs keep their teeth clean.

# Puppies

A **litter** of golden retrievers may have about eight puppies. The puppies are born blind and deaf. They drink their mother's milk. Puppies will begin seeing and hearing at about two weeks old.

Puppies should stay with their mother for eight weeks. Golden retrievers may live as long as 12 years.

A golden retriever with puppies.

# Dogs With Jobs

Some people train golden retrievers for special jobs. Some learn to be search dogs. Search dogs use their keen sense of smell to find people. They find people that are lost or trapped. Search dogs also help police find criminals.

Some golden retrievers learn to help people with disabilities. Some pull wheelchairs. Some open and close doors for people. Service dogs guide blind people, too.

Some service dogs help people who cannot see.

# Important Words

**breed**  a special group of dogs. Dogs of the same breed look alike.

**diet**  the food that a dog (or a person) normally eats.

**groom**  to clean and care for.

**litter**  the group of puppies born at one time.

**veterinarian**  a doctor for animals. A short name for veterinarian is "vet."

# Web Sites

To learn more about golden retrievers, visit ABDO Publishing Company on the World Wide Web. Web sites about golden retrievers are featured on our Book Links page. These links are routinely monitored and updated to provide the most current information available.

## www.abdopub.com

# Index

American Kennel Club
  **6, 8**

baths **14**

breed **5, 6, 8**

brushing **13**

Canidae family **4**

chew toys **18**

coat **10, 13, 14**

cocker spaniels **6**

dingoes **4**

ears **14**

exercise **16, 17**

food **15**

foxes **4**

greyhounds **6**

jackals **4**

litter **19**

nails **14**

North America **8**

puppies **19, 20**

Scotland **6**

search dogs **21**

service dogs **22**

teeth **14, 18**

Tweedmouth, Lord **6**

veterinarian **14**

wolves **4**